Praise for *Women*

'As always, Paula Gooder makes us see the biblical text
with fresh eyes and challenges us to see beyond our lazy
and stereotyping reading. Each beautifully-written and
illustrated reflection vividly highlights a particular
woman's encounter with Jesus; each one is firmly rooted in
the text, and reminds us to keep noticing, as Jesus did,
the people that we might think of as marginal, but whom
Jesus sees as at the very heart of the gospel.'

DR JANE WILLIAMS
McDonald Professor in Theology, St Mellitus College

'Giving a voice to the voiceless is something that
Paula Gooder does with amazing effect in this book.
From the sidelines these nine women are brought into
the centre of the drama of Holy Week and we are
the beneficiaries of the stories that they tell.'

THE VERY REVD ANDREW NUNN
Dean of Southwark

Paula Gooder is a writer and lecturer in Biblical Studies. She is the author of many popular books, including *Phoebe: A Story* (2018) and *The Parables* (2020), and one of the editors of the *Pilgrim Course*. Paula is also Canon Chancellor of St Paul's Cathedral, London.

Ally Barrett has worked in theological education as well as parish ministry and enjoys working at the intersection of creativity, faith, wellbeing and sustainability. She is the author of several books and dozens of hymns. Ally is Chaplain of St Catharine's College, Cambridge.

Women of Holy Week

An Easter journey in nine stories

Paula Gooder

with illustrations by Ally Barrett

CHURCH HOUSE
PUBLISHING

Text © Paula Gooder 2022
Illustrations © Ally Barrett 2022

Church House Publishing
Church House
Great Smith Street
London SW1P 3AZ

Published 2022 by Church House Publishing

Email: copyright@churchofengland.org

British Library Cataloguing in Publication Data

A catalogue record for this book is available from the British Library

ISBN 978 1 78140 289 4

Design and typesetting by www.penguinboy.net

Digital Photography by Daniel Barrett

Contents

Easter Day

Ascension Day

NOTES AND RESOURCES

Introduction

THESE NINE STORIES about nine different, but interlinked, women were written as Holy Week, Easter and Ascension Day reflections for Southwark Cathedral in 2021.

Holy Week is a time when Christians across the world travel together as companions on the way in reflection and in prayer, focused on Jesus, the one whose suffering and death, whose resurrection and new life draws us together and makes us one. It is together, as God's people, that we accompany Jesus in this last week of his life, and as we do so we join countless others who have trod this way before us. One of the powerful features of Holy Week and Easter is that our remembrance of the events in the last week of Jesus' life joins us with those who were there with him and invites us to imagine what it might have been like to have seen the events for ourselves.

A few years ago, I was reflecting on this task of imagination, of placing ourselves in our minds into the story of Jesus and the early Church. As I reflected, I noticed something that brought me up short. When I imagined Jesus and his disciples, the early Church and the earliest followers, nearly everyone was a man. There was hardly a woman in sight. You may be thinking to yourself that there is a reason for this. The New Testament encourages us in this direction. The stories and discussions, the Gospels and Epistles have what you might call a strongly male cast. There are not many roles for women. And yet they were there: sometimes named, sometimes not; sometimes speaking, often silent.

You may be familiar with the Bechdel test in fiction and film. To pass the test two female characters need to have a conversation of a reasonable length about a subject other than a man. Only 50 per cent of contemporary films usually pass the test – we can, I'm sure, all agree that the Bible as a whole, let alone the Gospels, would not fare well under this scrutiny. Over the course of the past few years, however, I have tried to repopulate my own biblical imagination with women. Women who were there but whom we often miss, or simply forget. In these stories I have tried to draw attention to the women who were there, lurking in the background of the stories, key characters but often overlooked.

Over the course of the nine stories, I have imagined what it might have been like to accompany Jesus in this final week of his life from the perspective of nine women. Some of them we know with certainty were there because the Gospels tell us they were: the widow with two coins, the woman with the ointment of pure nard, Mary wife of Clopas, Mary Magdalene, Mary mother of Jesus. Some are not mentioned at all, but someone like them was probably present: a woman journeying to Jerusalem for the Passover, the wife of a scribe, and a female disciple at the Last Supper. I have also aimed to travel from the outside in: from people who had the most fleeting encounters with Jesus at the start of the week to his most devoted followers at the end.

With each story, I have provided one or more Bible passages that can be read alongside the stories, and a few questions to prompt reflection and conversation. In addition, for each story I have provided a few additional notes which you might find helpful to aid you in your own inhabiting of the events.

About
the Paintings
Ally Barrett

ILLUSTRATING A BOOK means creating images that are in conversation with the words. The book's audience can then be drawn into that conversation, bringing with them their own thoughts, questions, experiences and perspectives.

For me, making paintings to illustrate a theological text is a process of theological reflection. The way in which an image responds to the text and its scriptural underpinnings can sometimes draw attention to questions and resonances that might otherwise have gone unnoticed. In both image and word there is also potential for playfulness as well as depth in referencing larger theological themes.

Many of these stories take place at liminal – or in-between – times, especially the beginnings and ends of the day. This impacts how light and shadow works both pictorially and theologically. I've tried to use the paintings to show how the encounters captured in the stories enjoy a radiance that comes not from a natural light source but from the presence of God in that particular Kairos moment. We might reflect, as we read, on how the text illuminates our experience, and how our experience and perspective spotlights particular aspects of a story, asking ourselves: 'Where is God in this?'

Above all, I wanted these images to reflect the interconnectedness of the stories. Developing the ancient triple form of the triptych, the individual images form a three by three square. We begin at the top left corner, moving clockwise round in a spiral, and ending in the centre. (You can see a large version of the full *Women of Holy Week* cycle in the middle of Mary Mother of Jesus' Story on pages 60–61.) The stories and images culminate in the moment that Christ becomes embodied in the faithful at Pentecost, gathered around Mary herself, in whose own body Jesus was formed and grown.

The spiral shape of the whole is suggested in the composition and contours of each image. Often angles, lines, shadows, colours and even objects transcend the boundary of their own square and visit their neighbouring squares - just as Anna visits Sarah and Jacob. This might serve as a reminder that we are called to look beyond our own 'box' as we learn to see Christ in one another.

I hope you enjoy these images alongside Paula's wonderful words. And I also hope you might consider making your own images, either through art or through imagination. As you engage with the stories and reflect on your own Kairos moments of encounter, I hope you will find ways to paint or write your story into the bigger story of God's limitless love for the world.

Palm
Sunday

The First Woman

Miriam's
Story

MY NAME IS MIRIAM. I come from Sepphoris in Galilee where I live with my family. We're fish traders. It's a good life. Selling fish to the Romans turns a steady profit.

The money is good. The weather is glorious – rarely too hot or too cold. Our life is peaceful. We in Sepphoris know what's good for us: we're loyal to Rome and Rome leaves us alone. Not like those mad fanatics in the hills. They'll get themselves killed one day, mark my words.

Don't get me wrong. I'd love to see the back of those Romans as much as anyone. When the Messiah comes (and I know he will), I'll be the first to cheer on his army as they kick out the Romans. But until he does come, I'll keep my head down and mind my own business. I'll leave the Romans alone and hope they leave me alone. That way no harm could possibly come to anyone … could it?

THIS YEAR, LIKE EVERY YEAR, we've come to Jerusalem for the Passover. Us and most of the rest of Galilee. I love it and hate it all at the same time. I love the excitement and the expectation; I hate the smell and the jostling. I love the togetherness of us all in the same place for the same reason; I hate the fights that erupt at a moment's notice. I love going to the Temple to meet my God; I hate being pushed out of the way by those people who think they've a better right to be there than I have.

I especially love that moment when all the crowds who have been travelling from north and south and east and west join together as we stream into Jerusalem. And as we go we sing. We sing as though our hearts would burst within in us. We sing the ancient tunes of the psalms, voices of strangers mingling together, weaving us together as one as we sing our way into the Holy City, the City of God. One of my favourites of these psalms has always been 'The Song of Victory': *'O give thanks to the LORD, for he is good: his steadfast love endures for ever.'*

When we pilgrims sing it, the sound of it ripples backwards and forwards down the long line of people: *'His steadfast love endures for ever ... endures for ever ... for ever ... and ever ... and ever.'*

This year we started singing that psalm, my favourite psalm, just as we got to Bethany. The timing couldn't have been more perfect. It's a psalm all about a king – a king who really existed. When we sing this psalm, I love to imagine him, weary and bruised from battle, coming to Jerusalem exhausted but quietly triumphant. Riding down the very road I'm on now, remembering the struggle and the battle and how he was nearly lost but how the steadfast love of the Lord really does endure for ever. And he was saved. And how the priests would stream out of the Temple to greet him singing, *'Blessed is the one who comes in the name of the LORD'* – and there would be joy and thanksgiving everywhere. One day – one day we'll sing this for real when the Messiah, our new king, comes. When he's driven the

Romans out and there's peace and justice everywhere, then we'll sing this with all our might. *'Blessed is the one who comes in the name of the LORD.'*

I was thinking about that – as I always do on the way to Jerusalem – when two people brought a donkey, and a man got on it. It was strange, almost as though he'd expected it somehow. He rode it – just like I always imagined the king would have done – except that it was a donkey and not that impressive. The crowd parted for a moment and I recognized some of them around him from the fish market back home. There was Peter and his brother – the quiet one (I think his name was Andrew). And Zebedee's boys who'd upped and offed a few years ago leaving their poor father to do all the work. I heard that they'd gone off after one of those wannabe Messiah types. Then I saw the man on the donkey himself. He should have looked ridiculous but somehow he didn't. He looked – well … right. Kingly and gentle, powerful and caring all rolled into one. Just like I imagined steadfast love would look.

Someone pushed a branch into my hand as we got close to the end of the psalm. I found myself singing and waving my branch, 'Save us, Hosanna! Save us.' All around me people were doing the same, singing directly to the man on the donkey as though our very lives depended on it: *'Save us, Hosanna! Save us. Blessed is the one who comes in the name of the LORD.'* In that moment it felt as though he really could – save us, that is.

He couldn't be The One, could he? No, of course not. The Romans are all around us. Look at them twitching for the merest chance to draw their swords. In any case, he doesn't look the part – not even approaching magnificent enough to be a proper Messiah.

And the priests haven't come out of the Temple to greet him. If it was him, they'd know, wouldn't they? Priests are trained to recognize the things of God. If he really was the Messiah they'd know and they'd tell us. Then we'd all know. No Messiah would leave it to chance, would they?

I KEPT HOLD OF MY BRANCH, just in case. Just in case the priests suddenly came to meet him like they ought to. But nothing happened. No one came. The moment went just as quickly as it had arrived. I let my branch fall to the ground, strangely disappointed.

He wasn't anything like I'd hoped the Messiah would be and yet … and yet I couldn't help thinking that if the Messiah comes – when the Messiah comes – wouldn't the world be so much better if, instead of being magnificent and grand, powerful and splendid, he was like this man: steadfast love in human form.

We came to the end of the psalm, the final verse echoing off the walls of the city: *'O give thanks to the LORD for he is good: his steadfast love endures for ever … endures for ever … for ever … and ever … and ever.'*

The Second Woman

Sarah's
Story

MY NAME IS SARAH. I'm here in Jerusalem for the Passover. I came with my husband Jacob, though I won't see much of him while he's here. He's a priest and can trace his heritage all the way back to Aaron. If you ever meet him, don't ask him about it – really, don't. When I say he can trace his heritage back, he really can. Given half a chance he will tell you about it, ancestor by ancestor, until you wish you'd never asked.

We live in Sepphoris in Galilee for most of the year. Two weeks each year, Jacob comes up to Jerusalem to do his priestly service. At those times he comes on his own, but for the three big festivals – Passover, Pentecost and Tabernacles – I come, too. Who wouldn't? There's no time like it.

It's a bit of a squeeze. Human beings crammed into every conceivable space. But who wouldn't want to be here at this most holy time of year? In the moment when we remember our freedom, who we really are as God's people. Even those Romans lurking everywhere can do nothing to dampen our memory of freedom. God freed us once and will do it again, and again, as often as we have need of it. No wonder they don't like us all cramming into the city. What oppressing army would feel happy with millions of people getting together to remember freedom?

THE WEIRDEST THING HAPPENED TODAY. I was coming back from the market when I bumped into Miriam. I get my fish from her in Sepphoris. When I say I bumped into her, I bumped right into her. The streets were crammed as they always are once the pilgrims arrive, and she was walking along like she was in a dream. The crowd swept us along as we tried to talk. I couldn't hear everything she said. Something about a man. She'd seen him in the pilgrim procession yesterday, riding a donkey of all ridiculous things. And he wasn't the Messiah, except she'd hoped he was, but he can't have been. Jesus, she thought his name was. But now she couldn't stop thinking about him. I'd just asked her why, when the crowd surged around us and she got carried away in one direction and me in another. On the air, I just heard *'steadfast love'* and *'for ever'*. And then she was gone.

Miriam is one of those down-to-earth types. Doesn't get carried away with anything (other than a nice big Galilean tilapia fish). So I was thinking about her and wondering what had happened to her when I returned to our rented guest room to find Jacob there. He'd just met a rabbi. He'd heard about him, apparently – he'd been making quite a stir in Galilee, especially Capernaum. But he'd never been to Sepphoris and so Jacob had never met him. Jesus, his name was. I started. I know it's a common name but it was the second time I'd heard it in an hour. Could this really be the same person?

'Where was he?' I asked.

As soon as the question left my mouth, I knew what

the answer would be. Where else would Jacob have met him but in the Temple? Around the festivals Jacob barely left the Temple. He needed to be there for his duties – the thousands upon thousands of lambs that needed sacrificing (how he stomached the stench I will never know, half an hour was enough for me), the daily worship, the prayers and the singing. But even when he didn't need to be there, he was there. Poring over the Scriptures and the teaching of the rabbis, debating and arguing often late into the night. Jacob loved the law as much as he loved life itself – more, probably. Jacob would have said that the law was life itself. He loved that psalm – the very first one – about studying the law being like a tree standing by a river. He was like a tree, my Jacob, strong and secure, but able to bend in the wind when he needed to.

THIS JESUS, WHO JACOB HAD MET, had been in the Temple. After his duties were over, Jacob had gone, as he loved to, to the Stoa, where people loved to gather and talk. As Jacob had arrived that day, a group of high-ranking priests had stormed past. Muttering something about needing to get rid of him, and as soon as possible before he poisoned too many minds. A large crowd was gathered there and Jacob had headed to join it. Where there was a crowd there was debate; where there was debate there was study of the law, and my Jacob never missed that if he could help it.

In the middle of the crowd sat a man. A simple-looking

man, dressed like a peasant. The crowd seemed to be hanging on his every word. On the outskirts of the crowd people were still chuckling. Apparently this man – Jesus – had just told a bold and outrageous story about a vineyard with corrupt tenants who would do anything to hold on to what they didn't own. As the story went on, the whole crowd had known he was talking about the Sanhedrin and the Chief Priest. The last person to realize it was Caiaphas himself. By the time he did realize it, the whole crowd was reverberating with laughter. 'I thought Caiaphas was going to throttle him then and there,' wheezed Jacob's neighbour, gasping for breath because he had laughed so much.

Jacob had watched the man in the middle of the crowd, he told me. Jesus was now in deep in debate with a group of Sadducees and Jacob had watched fascinated. The Sadducees had set up a perfect problem – one of their favourites. Jacob had heard them do it before and it had defeated absolutely everyone. If you believe in resurrection – and Jacob hadn't decided yet if he did, he wasn't a Pharisee after all – but if you did believe in it the question was what would happen to a woman after the resurrection if she had had more than one husband? It was an impossible question – no one could answer it. But this Jesus did. Jacob thought that the Sadducees couldn't decide whether to be impressed or annoyed. In the end they'd settled on annoyed and stalked off.

'I'M NOT QUITE SURE WHAT CAME OVER ME,' said Jacob, who was normally excruciatingly shy. 'I pushed through the crowd and I asked him my question.'

'The first commandment?'

I smiled. It was Jacob's favorite conundrum. What's the first commandment? The first one given? Or the most important one? And if you had to choose, which one would you pick? However you answer it, you risk losing something really important from the law. Jacob and his friends could talk about it for hours.

'What did he say?'

'First you love God; second you love your neighbour.

Together they are the most important commandment all rolled into one.'

'You knew that already,' I said. 'Rabbi Hillel taught it to you.'

'He did, but not quite like this. For Rabbi Hillel it was a clever question that needed a clever answer. But this man Jesus said it like it was a truth to be lived. *Love God; love your neighbour*. It's the answer to everything. And looking at him, I knew he lived it with all his heart and soul and mind and strength. And then he looked at me and said,

"You are not far from the kingdom of God."'

'What did he mean?' I asked.

'I've no idea,' Jacob replied. 'It could mean lots of different things.'

I saw the gleam in Jacob's eye and I knew, without a shadow of a doubt, that he had a new favourite question.

The Third Woman
Anna's
Story

My name is Anna. I've lived in Jerusalem all my life. The Temple – God's Temple – has been the centre of my life for as long as I can remember. Wherever I go, the Temple is in the corner of my eye, helping me to navigate through Jerusalem's winding streets, reminding me that, no matter what happens, God, my God, is right there with me.

I was named after my great-aunt, Anna. She was a prophet and after her husband died she lived in the Temple day and night, fasting and praying and reading Scripture. She lived in a corner of the court of the women – as close as she was allowed to be to her God. She couldn't go further and even in her old age she harrumphed her indignation at it – at the thought that she, a small, bent old woman could in any way threaten her God, creator and judge of the whole world, whose steadfast love endures for ever but who might flee in fright if a woman got too close.

I used to go and visit her, and she would tell me the old, old stories of our faith. Of Abraham, Isaac and Jacob; of Sarah and Hagar, Rebekah and Rachel; of Moses and Joshua; of Zipporah and Rahab. At the end she would grasp my hands tightly and whisper, '*It's your story, too – never let them paint you out.*' And I would smile and nod, wondering what she meant.

One day, just after I was married, I arrived in the Temple to visit her as usual. As I entered the court of the women, one of the Levites drew me to one side.

'She's lost it,' he said. 'I think it's time you took her home.'

I looked over to the corner where she studied and prayed and slept, to see her, full of life, talking to a crowd of people. I looked at the Levite, questioningly.

'She thinks she's met the Messiah, bless her. She talks about him to anyone who'll listen. And best of all, she says he was a baby.' He laughed and returned to his post at the gate, shooing away some unsuspecting visiting Gentiles who had paused for long enough at the entrance to suggest that they thought they might come in.

I walked over to my great-aunt, slightly bemused. The previous week, when I visited her, she had shown no signs of the fading of her spirit that you sometimes see in elders. Quite the opposite – she was as sprightly and insightful as ever. She saw me walking towards her and hurried over as quickly as her bent frame would allow. (Those endless nights sleeping in the Temple had done her body no good at all.)

'Little Anna.' To her I would always be little Anna, even though I towered above her now.

'Little Anna,' she said, 'I saw him.'

'Who?' I asked, concerned, remembering the Levite's words.

'The Saviour. I held him in my arms. I sang him a lullaby – a love song for my Lord.'

A few days later she died and now, every time I go to the Temple, I look over into her corner and wonder who or what she thought she had seen. They told me later that she died with a smile on her lips whispering the words, '*the steadfast love of the LORD endures for ever*'.

TODAY AS I GOT READY TO GO THE TEMPLE, slowly and wearily, I wondered what Anna would say to me now. When she was alive, I faced life with joy and confidence. Thinking that nothing could bring me down. I was wrong. Life itself defeated me. God's very self brought me to the depths of the pit. I am left with nothing, only the echoes of my cries to a God who never answers.

A few years ago I had everything and now I gather everything I have left in the world to go to the Temple to make my gift.

I know I don't have to. I'm 'only' a woman. No one expects me to. No one cares especially. No one notices if I do.

Until this year, I'd have said that God notices. The God who has loved me from the moment I was woven together in my mother's womb; the God who sees my sitting down and my rising; the God whom great-aunt Anna loved with every fibre of her being.

Until this year, I'd have said that that God sees.

But last year, almost exactly to the day, a mysterious illness crept through the city, taking first my parents, then my sons and, last of all, my husband.

And now I am alone – quite alone – in the world.

I have no money.

Well, that's not strictly speaking true. I have two coins. Tiny, they are – the size of my thumbnail.

One to buy bread for tomorrow.

The last one I'll give in thanks to my God.

THE JOURNEY TO THE TEMPLE seemed longer than usual. I was jostled at every step. I almost gave up. The joy of the pilgrims seemed to mock my numb misery.

At last I stood before the funnels of the treasury. At the next funnel was a man who had come with his whole family. Seven sons, he had. I know that because he announced it so loudly.

'I've come to pay the Temple tax for myself and my seven sons,' he proclaimed as he dropped eight, gleaming silver half-shekels, one by one, from a great height into the bronze funnel in front of him.

'God is good,' he declared at full volume. And then, under his breath, thinking no one could hear him, 'And so am I.'

He turned to walk away, barging into me as he did so. When he saw me, he dusted himself down, disgust written all over his face. I wanted to tell him, I wasn't always like this. I wanted to tell him that I used to come with my husband and sons and pay the Temple tax in full just like him. I wanted him to see me not as I am now but as I used to be. But even as I opened my mouth to speak, I realized that words simply couldn't say all that needed to be said.

I turned to the treasury box. Its bronze mouth seemingly mocking the smallness and inadequateness of my gift. I stood there for a moment, looking at those two tiny coins. All I had left in the world, held in the palm of my hand. As I stood there, I could have sworn I heard Anna's voice echoing in my ear: *'His steadfast love endures for ever.'*

Before I knew what I'd done, I dropped both coins into the funnel – my love-gift for the God who, despite it all, I had to believe saw me and loved me. The sound of their double clink echoed round the courtyard.

I looked instinctively in the direction of Anna's corner. There was a man standing there, surrounded by a group of people. He looked right at me; right – or so it felt – into my numb, grieving heart. He simply nodded at me and turned to say something to those around him. I could see from his eyes that *he* saw me, saw all of it. He turned to those around him and pointed at me, his eyes full of admiration.

WHEN I GOT HOME, standing outside my tiny room was my neighbour of a few days. She told me she was called Sarah, and that (along with her husband Jacob, a priest) she was here for the feast. She wondered, she said, if I'd like to eat with them while they were here. They had plenty to share.

'But why?' I stammered. 'Why would you do that for me?'

She smiled at me and said, "'Love God and love your neighbour, that is the whole law." Someone said that to my husband recently – someone who meant it with the whole of themselves. And it makes more sense to me than anything else I've ever heard.'

Suddenly I felt an overwhelming need to lean against the wall for strength. Could it be? Could it be that the God who sees had heard my cry after all?

The Fourth Woman
Susannah's Story

M Y NAME IS SUSANNAH. I grew up in Caesarea Maritima, right on the coast. Our villa looked out over the sea, its bluey-green light stretching as far as the eye could see.

As a child, I had no idea how lucky I was. Our family had more than enough money. I had a mother and father who loved me. We lived in an elegant, spacious house. I had beautiful clothes. I wanted for nothing.

On the day of my betrothal my father gave me an alabaster jar. It was the most beautiful thing I had ever seen. White with ripples of a sandy colour that ran over its smooth surface. It was cool and heavy in my hand. My father put his hand affectionately on my cheek.

'Something precious for the most precious person I know. Open it on a special occasion, dear one.'

NOT LONG AFTERWARDS I went to live in my husband's equally elegant house in Tiberias. And very soon I learnt how lucky I used to be.

My husband Alexander was rich, very rich, a courtier of Herod Antipas. On the surface he was charming; underneath he was nasty. Cruelty was a sport for him. He used to boast of his love of tormenting people. He would find their weak spot and press and press until they broke. There was a particular gleam that would shine in his eye then, as though the act of destruction thrilled him. Soon after, he would seek out a new victim and begin again.

And so the special occasion for opening my father's precious gift never really came. On days when the spite and the cruelty had worn me down, I would hold its cool smoothness in my hand and remember the time when I had known myself to be loved and cherished. And then I would place it carefully back on the shelf, a memento of a life long gone.

Eventually, as I knew it always would, my husband's cruel gaze landed on me. He was bored one day and was looking for a victim. I think he was probably bored of me, too. Antipas had just divorced his first wife to marry his half-brother's wife, Herodias. So divorce was all the rage at court. He could just have cast me off, but that wasn't Alexander's style.

My weak spot wasn't hard to find. My love for my home and my parents shone through me with every breath, and so he set about making sure that after he'd done with me I could never go back. He started rumours, claiming that I was an adulteress three times, four times over. People love to believe the worst of someone, and in no time at all my reputation was in tatters. Branded a sinner, I was cast into the street, unable to go home lest I bring down shame on my father.

What Alexander hadn't counted on in all his cruelty, however, was that others were different.

My father couldn't receive me – a proclaimed sinner – back into his house, but he could still take care of me. He sent money via Joanna, the wife of Herod's steward, so I was comfortable – a famous, despised but wealthy sinner.

ONE DAY, JOANNA AND HER FRIEND Mary from Magdala came to find me. They had met a man, a rabbi, they said, and I *had* to meet him. I flinched.

'I can't meet a rabbi! I'm a sinner, he'll know. I can't even meet my own father; how can I meet a rabbi?'

'You'll see,' said Mary.

So I went with them reluctantly, every nerve in my body ready to flee at the merest hint that I'd been recognized. Mary and Joanna, sensing this, kept a firm grip on my arms, almost carrying me there. When we reached the house where Jesus was, there was a group outside: priests and Levites and Pharisees, muttering and gesticulating their outrage. I tensed. It wouldn't be long before they worked out who I was and drove me away. But they were so intent on their outrage that I passed right by without them even noticing.

Inside the house, in the gloom, I glanced around in astonishment. This was not what I expected. Gathered there were ordinary people, traders and farmers, daily labourers and – wait – surely not some tax collectors?

The crowd willingly moved up to let us in. At that moment Jesus looked straight at me.

'Dear child,' he said, 'your sins are forgiven.'

I opened my mouth to tell him that it wasn't my fault, that Alexander had made it all up. I wanted to tell him all my hurt and my anger and my loneliness but, instead, found myself looking into his eyes. As I did, I knew that I was deeply and utterly loved, just as I am.

I didn't need to explain. I didn't need to justify anything. I didn't need to be caught in Alexander's web of accusation and cruelty any more. In an instant it was gone. I was free.

THAT DAY I BEGAN FOLLOWING HIM, with the twelve and a number of others, Mary and Joanna included. We used the money we had to help out, to pay for food and lodging when he needed it.

Then a few days ago we came to Jerusalem. Jesus and the twelve slept out on the sloping banks of the olive groves just below Bethany. Mary and Joanna and a few other women, including Jesus' mother Mary, found rooms in the city. This morning, as I left my room, for some reason I felt in the bottom of my bag and pulled out my most precious possession: the alabaster jar. I stood there looking at it for a few moments.

Just then, two women came out of the next-door room, laughing as they went. I'd met them when we first arrived. One was called Sarah and, like us, had come over from Jerusalem where she was staying for the festival. The other was Anna. Her face told a tragic tale of loss and grief and loneliness. But today her eyes danced. She touched my hand briefly and gently.

'Love extravagantly, dear,' she said, 'with your whole heart and soul and mind and strength.'

All of a sudden, I knew the special day had come.

I RAN UP THE HILL TO BETHANY, arriving sweaty and out of breath.

I had to push my way into the room where they were all dining. Jesus was in the place of honour, so I had to walk past them all to get to him. Before I'd have been crippled by the shame of it. But not now. Not today.

All those years I'd held on to the bottle, I'd never asked myself how to open it. You were meant to use it a few drops at a time so it must have a lid. Oh, what did it matter? I was going to pour it all out anyway.

So I smashed it, a sense of joyful elation bubbling around me as I did, and I poured it out.

I poured it all over his head. I poured out my love and my gratitude. I poured out my joy and my freedom. I poured out my very self all over his head. It was an act of absurdity, but I knew that he would understand.

The oil ran down his hair and his cheeks, down his beard and his neck, getting in his eyes and his ears as it went, so he had to rub it away with his sleeve and then his other sleeve. Its pungent smell filled the air.

You could hear the muttering swirl around the room as one by one they realized that the jar contained pure nard. *'Is she mad? That's a year's wages wasted. Just think of all the poor she could have helped. Someone should do something.'*

Jesus looked right at me and winked. His enjoyment of

what I'd just done written all over his face.

'Oh, leave her alone,' he said. 'Today, she has anointed my body for burial. I tell you, wherever good news is proclaimed in all the world, what she has done will be told in memory of her.'

I skirted the outside of the room as I headed to the door, a warm glow in my heart. Jesus had received my ridiculous, extravagant gift exactly as I had hoped that he might – better even.

He'd said it would be remembered. He said I would be remembered and talked about for ever.

I didn't understand what he meant about burial – I've never seen anyone look more alive. But he often said things I didn't understand. I stored it away to think about later.

I could hear them talking about me as I left.

'What was her name again?' asked one of them.

'Don't know. Mary, I think?' said another.

Maundy Thursday

The Fifth Woman
Joanna's Story

Y NAME IS JOANNA. I live with my husband Chuza in Tiberias. Chuza is Herod Antipas' steward. He loves the life. He loves the court intrigue and the power. He loves being at the centre of Herod's web – pulling strings, controlling everything that happens, plotting and winning.

He especially loves winning.

He's not a bad man, or at least he didn't used to be. Not like Susannah's husband – who was cruel from the start – my Chuza used to be kind and loving and thoughtful. But I barely see him these days. He loves court life; I hate it. There's not much more to say than that.

A FEW YEARS AGO, I MET JESUS, Jesus of Nazareth. Court life had been suffocating me, draining me of life. So I paid a fisherman to let me ride in his boat across the sea of Galilee to Capernaum. And there he was. In a boat on the edge of the lake, talking to a huge crowd. He told a story about a sower sowing seeds; some growing and others not. It felt in that moment as though something was sown in me. I just had to know more.

So I began to follow him, me and a number of women. First, Mary from Magdala, then Susannah – after her husband threw her out – then Salome, and Mary, Clopas' wife, and Mary, James and Joses' mother. And Mary and Martha – not to forget the other Mary, Jesus' mother, and her sister. Most people didn't notice we were there. In years to come I don't imagine they will even remember we were there. But we were, and we are. Following – just as much as Peter and Andrew, James and John and the others.

This year we all came to Jerusalem for the Passover. We don't normally all come together, but this year feels different somehow. It feels as though there's some kind of shadow hanging over us all, just out of sight, but hanging there nevertheless. Recently Jesus has started saying the strangest things – about the Son of Man needing to suffer and be rejected and die and rise again. None of us had any idea what he meant. But when he said it, there would be a look of such devastating sadness in his eyes, I thought my heart would break.

One time I told him we didn't understand. He looked at me with such love in his eyes and said, 'You will. One day, you will.'

I'VE BEEN WORRYING FOR DAYS about Passover. Once the pilgrims flood into the city you can't get a decent-sized room for love nor money. And there were so many of us. Jesus and the twelve, and us women and a few others besides. I kept on asking the other disciples but they didn't seem that bothered about it. I even tried talking to Judas but he seemed distracted – had done for days. Getting two words out of him together was nigh on impossible.

At last I broke down. I couldn't bear it a moment longer and I burst out:

'So where do you want us to go and make the

preparations for you to eat the Passover?

I realized it sounded unnecessarily aggressive, but by then I was so frustrated I didn't know where to put myself.

He laughed – in that way that he had – throwing his head back and shaking with mirth.

'You could just have asked!' he said.

He told me to go with Susannah. We'd find a man with a water jar, he said. He'd take us to a house where we were to say, 'The Teacher is asking for the guest room.'

So we did. And it worked exactly like he'd said. The man took us up the outside stairs to the roof, where tables and reclining couches were set up already. All around us – on roofs across the city – others were preparing themselves for the feast, and in the distance the Temple stood proudly against the skyline.

Throughout the day, one by one, the other women arrived and soon our preparations were in full swing.

As night fell, Jesus arrived with the twelve. We all settled down together to eat and drink and remember our story, a story of freedom and of a God who hears our cry. Towards the end of the meal, Jesus picked up a loaf of bread – just like he always did at the start of every meal. He raised his eyes to heaven and blessed it and passed it round.

'This is my body,' he said.

We looked at each other, flummoxed. It was one of those many moments of late where we had to admit we didn't really know what was going on. It was bread. What on earth did he mean?

'Take, eat,' he said. 'This is my body, given for you.'

Then he took a cup.

'This is my blood of the new covenant, poured out for many. Drink it,' he prompted.

So we did. Not understanding, but feeling, somehow, as though this moment would define us for the rest of our lives.

Jesus was like that, I'd found over the years: he would let you grow into the truth that he brought in your own time. There was no judgement; no condemnation if you didn't understand. Just when you were ready was fine with him.

I couldn't shake the feeling, though, that this time, time was short. That I needed to work it out urgently. I knew this Jesus had changed the world for ever. I knew he was our long-awaited Messiah. I knew, even, that long-expected though he had been, so far he had defied every expectation we had.

All this I knew. But there was something – something I didn't know. It lurked just out of reach at the edges of my mind. I reached for it desperately, but it slipped further away.

Just then, Jesus and the twelve got up to go. No, I was wrong. Someone was missing. Where on earth was Judas? I'm sure he was here before. The feeling of unease I'd had all evening lurched into a feeling of dread.

Something was wrong. Something was very wrong.

I asked Peter about it. But he wasn't the most perceptive of people even at the best of times.

'It's fine,' he said. 'We've had a busy few days and we're tired. We'll have a nap when we get to Gethsemane and everything will look better tomorrow.'

I tried to explain to him my sense of looming disaster, but I didn't even understand it myself so how could I begin to put it into words?

'Get some sleep,' he said. 'You worry too much.'

It's true, I do. But this time I feared I wasn't worrying enough.

Jesus turned at the top of the stairs and looked at each of us in turn. He raised his hand in greeting and turned to go.

A low moan next to me made me turn in just enough time to catch Jesus' mother as she dropped to her knees. We sat there, together, we women. Grieving for the disaster – whatever it was – that was coming.

'That's the problem with extravagant love,' whispered Susannah. 'It brings with it extravagant heartbreak.'

We huddled together on the rooftop, the Temple outline stark on the horizon.

It was going to be a long night.

Good
Friday

The Sixth Woman
Salome's Story

MY NAME IS SALOME. I know what you're thinking – not that Salome.

I grew up in Nazareth with Mary. We were inseparable – until the angel came. Not that I knew at the time that an angel had come.

One day we were young women facing the future together; the next, Mary just stopped talking to me. Then the gossip started: she was pregnant and it wasn't Joseph's. No one knew why Joseph stood by her. She'd brought shame right into his house but still he protected her. It made no sense to anyone. They were the talk of the village. They went away for the census and I didn't see her for years.

Then one day, years later, she and Joseph returned with their little boy Jesus. They'd been in Egypt, apparently. Years went by, the gossip subsided, and we became close again.

I remember so clearly when Jesus started to travel and teach – Mary was mortified. After being in the spotlight all those years she had imagined a quiet old age, her family around her. It took her a while but eventually she understood and she'd reminisce about the strange events that happened at his birth. She'd always known, she said, that he wouldn't be just anybody. She just hadn't wanted to accept it.

At first, I kept up with what he was doing for Mary's sake, but before long I followed him for my own sake. His teaching made sense of the world – it made sense of me.

So, I was there on that awful day. We were there … people often forget it, but we were there.

LATER THEY SAID THAT all his followers had run away. That he had been left alone – quite alone. That everyone had left him.

'Everyone?' I would ask.

'Yes, we all left him,' Peter would say. 'We're all as bad as each other. We all left him. We all fled.'

'All of us?'

'Yes, all of us. Every last … Oh.'

It often took him a while but most of the time he would get there in the end – at least until he forgot again.

'Not everyone.'

'Exactly,' I would say. 'Not everyone.'

YOU SEE, WE WERE THERE, Mary Magdalene and me. Obviously not in the Garden of Gethsemane: Jesus had gone ahead with the twelve by himself, leaving us bemused and grieving on the roof. But the moment we heard what had happened – and it went round Jerusalem like wildfire – we followed him. Just like we had in happier times in Galilee.

It's what I've always done. When disaster strikes and I

don't know what to do, I do what I normally do – day in, day out – until the moment comes when I do know what to do again. So, when we heard, when it felt as though the world was collapsing around us, we did what we had been doing for the past few years.

We followed him.

We followed him to Caiaphas' house and shivered through the long dark hours in the courtyard. We followed him to Pilate's house, listening with incredulous horror while the crowd cried out, 'Crucify, crucify!' all around us. We followed him to Herod's house (and back again).

And then we followed him where we never imagined we'd go – to his crucifixion.

At some point during the long, miserable wait, Mary Magdalene slipped away and came back with the other women: Susannah and Joanna, Mary, Clopas' wife, and Mary, Joses' mother, and of course Jesus' own mother, Mary. It was pitch black by then, so we inched closer and closer, and we stood there.

We stood there all that cold, wretched day, watching, as – breath by dying breath – our hopes and dreams died before our eyes; and with them everything we held dear.

WE HAD TALKED OVER THE YEARS, Mary and I, about the strange events that had happened when he was born. In the end she told me about the angel coming. She even told me his name: Gabriel.

We pondered together about it all, wondering what it all meant. The thing we talked about most was what Simeon had said to her when she'd taken Jesus to the Temple as a baby. He said the strangest things about who Jesus would become, the outrage he would cause and how he would reveal who people really were. He was right – I'd seen it in so many of the people that Jesus met. I'd noticed it in myself. There was something about him, about him and how that made you react, which simply revealed who you really were – even if you weren't aware of it at all.

But it was the last thing that Simeon had said that Mary puzzled over the most. Apparently he'd turned to her at the end, looked at her with deep compassion and said that a sword would pierce her soul, too.

She'd wondered over the years what he'd meant. Perhaps he'd meant that awful moment when she'd thought Jesus was lost in Jerusalem. Perhaps he'd meant the pain of him leaving home, the desperate loss of her beloved firstborn son. Perhaps he'd meant the embarrassment she'd felt when she'd first heard that he had started teaching people without ever having studied with a rabbi first.

Was that what he'd meant?

We'd wondered together over many, many hours. As I stood there that day and looked at Mary then, I imagined that all those things we'd talked about felt like nothing more than pinpricks right now. As we were holding on to each other in our grief in a simple effort to stay upright, I discovered that she'd been thinking exactly the same thing. I heard her whisper quietly to herself: 'So this is what Simeon meant.'

AT SOME POINT DURING THAT LONG, lonely vigil, the beloved disciple appeared quietly by our side. I don't know when he got there. That was just like him. Never with a fanfare. Never drawing attention to himself. Never forcing himself into situations. I think that was what Jesus liked so much about him. His company was gentle, undemanding, easy. When so many people wanted so much from Jesus all of the time, he didn't. He was just there. He was one of those people: you felt better simply because they were there.

From the cross, Jesus noticed him at almost the same time we did. Jesus hadn't spoken during that long, agonizing time, but just then he said, 'Your son' and 'Your mother', looking at one and then the other of them. Then he just looked at Mary. A look of pure love. It broke my heart … and he wasn't even my son. A few moments later he asked for a drink and sighed, 'It is finished.'

Then it was. Everything was over; everything bar our anguish. We stood there for what felt like hours, numb and shocked.

Then we did what we'd always done: we followed him. Some men we didn't know took his body off the cross –

so we followed them. They took him to a tomb nearby – so we followed them. We watched as they buried him. They didn't anoint him or use spices – they were in too much of a rush before sundown. They put his body on the ledge, rolled the stone across the entrance and went away.

We stood at a distance, unsure what to do next. We couldn't do anything the next day – it was the Sabbath – but we agreed we'd come back early on Sunday morning, before anyone else was up. We would anoint him then. You may be thinking that we hadn't thought it through, and you'd be right. Grief does that to you. We had no idea how we'd roll the stone away. The whole task – not just the rolling of the stone but the anointing and the ceremony – all of it was a man's job really. Normally, our job was to lead the lamentation.

But we had no choice. They'd run away, all of them, and there was only us. And after everything he'd been through, after everything we'd been through, we couldn't bear the thought that his body would be left there uncared for, unwept over, unanointed.

We were doing what we'd always done: following him; caring for him as best we could, even when no one noticed.

THEY SAID LATER THAT EVERYONE RAN AWAY, but we were there. People often forget it, but we were there.

Easter
Eve

Mary
Magdalene's
Story

MY NAME IS MARY. I come from Magdala on the shores of the Sea of Galilee. Until Herod Antipas built Tiberias, Magdala was the biggest and richest city for miles around. My father used to love to say he was a farmer, and he was, of sorts – if you count strolling around his three vineyards and two olive groves, issuing orders to the slaves and sending his hundred sheep out with their shepherds as farming.

I used to love watching the shepherd boys calling their sheep in the morning. The boys would come in the first light of dawn, ten or so of them, and stand outside the pen and call and call. The sheep would come flocking out, jostling around their shepherds, recognizing their voices and ready for the day's journey to find grass.

Then one day, when I woke up, the world felt different. I felt different. I felt hazy and distant, as though a veil had settled over my mind. I would walk for miles and miles, restless and ill at ease. They told me I had evil spirits in me, though even that I couldn't take in. I just wanted to be alone, far away from the noise and the clamour of people around me.

Once when I'd been out walking off my restlessness, I met a man sitting on the shores of the lake talking to a large crowd of people. Something came over me. I knew I was talking, shouting and shaking, though I'd no idea what I was saying, and then, all of a sudden, a wave of peace washed over me, the veil lifted and I was myself again. The man – Jesus they said his name was – smiled at me and signalled to the people around him that I should sit at his feet, like a real disciple. I held back for a moment – it wasn't seemly for a woman – but he signalled again and I couldn't resist, so I sat and I listened and listened with the whole of my being.

He was talking about being the good shepherd and calling his sheep, and them knowing his voice and following him. I smiled at that bit: I knew how true that was. But then when he'd talked about knowing the sheep by name and calling their names, I chuckled to myself. He'd clearly never been around sheep much. I mean, who in their right mind gives a sheep a name? It was a nice idea, though.

From that moment on I followed him, me and a number of other women, like Susannah and Joanna and a handful of other Marys.

So I was there when they killed him; we women clinging together in horror as the unthinkable happened before our eyes. We watched where they buried him – hastily because the sun had begun to dip below the horizon, announcing the start of the Sabbath day. We sat together that day, barely moving or speaking. The shock had rendered us senseless.

Then, as the sun dipped again, marking the end of the Sabbath, I sprang to life. We had to do something. We'd agreed between us that we would return to anoint his body for burial. My first thought was the others – the male disciples. Anointing a man's body after death was a man's job. Perhaps they would like to know where he was laid?

I found out where they were staying and hurried round.

'Who is it?' an anxious voice shouted in response to my frantic knocking.

'Mary from Magdala,' I answered. The door opened a crack.

'What are you doing here? They might find us.'

James' anxious face peered out

'Who?' I asked bemused.

'The Romans. They always kill the followers after the leader.'

I pushed my way in but soon saw there was little hope in it. The terror in the room was palpable. Peter sat in the corner, rocking and weeping.

'He's been like that ever since Thursday evening,' James said, sadly. 'We can't get a word out of him.'

I returned home disheartened, my mind spinning. How on earth was I going to find myrrh and aloes enough to anoint his body in a city I didn't live in?

When I got back, I told the others what had happened.

'I wish I'd kept my jar of nard now,' said Susannah, wretchedly, 'I had no idea we'd need it so soon.'

'Sweet girl,' Jesus' mother said from across the room, stirring herself from her grief-ridden stupor, 'You honoured him in life: no gift is greater than that. We will find the spices we need.'

She was right. We did. We spread out across the city, begging, borrowing and buying what we could. In the early morning, when we met together and compared our haul, we had (we thought) just about enough. We went, carrying large water jars between us to bathe his poor battered body before anointing it.

By the time we got near the place where the tomb was, the sun had just risen, casting eerie, early morning shadows over the whole area. We'd been talking as we went about how we'd move the stone that they'd rolled across the entrance.

'That's strange,' Salome said as we approached. 'The way the shadows fall make it look as though the stone has gone.'

We looked, all of us straining to see through the early morning light.

'That's because it has,' said James' mother.

Our footsteps faltered, but then started again: we couldn't bear to see what had happened now, but also we couldn't bear not to see.

We peeped in through the entrance and there, right inside the tomb – sitting as comfortable as you like – was a young man, his robe gleaming white.

'Don't be alarmed,' he said.

Salome let out a sound, halfway between a laugh and a scream.

'He is not here, he's been raised. Go tell the disciples – especially Peter – tell them that he's going ahead of them to Galilee.'

We turned and ran, we ran and ran and ran, dropping the water and the carefully gathered spices as we went, never pausing for breath until we reached the safety of our rented room.

IN THE END, I DID TELL PETER and the other disciple. I broke into his room weeping with the news of another disaster. Now, on top of everything, they'd taken his body as well. The shock of it was enough to jolt Peter from his misery and they ran back with me to see the empty tomb.

They got there first. Their legs were longer than mine. By the time I arrived panting and out of breath, they'd seen for themselves that his body was gone; the linen wrapping lying there empty. After they left I stood outside the tomb for a while, my eyes blinded with tears, wondering whether I could salvage some of the ointment we'd dropped in our terror a few hours earlier. I leant against the entrance and let my grief and my weariness take hold of me.

After a while I felt the overwhelming urge to look in the tomb one more time, so I bent and looked in. The young man had now been joined by someone else, and they were sitting at either end of the ledge.

'Why are you crying?' they asked.

I'd opened my mouth to answer, when a voice behind me asked the same question.

'Why are you crying?'

A tumble of words burst out of me. When I told people about this later I tidied up my words into a coherent, comprehensible sentence, but the reality is I babbled on a tide of tears and snot about 'my Lord' and 'his body' and 'it was gone' and 'I don't know where' and 'I didn't know what to do'.

He waited quietly for my gibbering to fade away and then he said just one word.

'Mary.'

The good shepherd had called my name, and I knew his voice with every fibre of my being.

Later, people would ask us – those of us who'd met the risen Christ – what he said that made us believe it was really him. Thomas would tell his story of Jesus' wounds and of being asked to put his hands in them. Peter would tell his story of Jesus asking if he loved him. And then they'd look at me. 'Mary met him first,' they'd say.

'What did he say to you?' they'd ask.

'He said "Mary",' I'd tell them.

'Is that all? Did he say anything else?'

They'd look a bit disappointed.

But I wasn't. Not for a moment.

Easter
Day

The Eighth Woman

Mary, Wife of
Clopas' Story

M Y NAME IS MARY. No, not the one you're thinking
of – not the mother of Jesus. And, no, not *that* one
either – not Mary Magdalene. There's so many of us Marys
and Miriams around, it's easy to get confused.

I am Mary – the one who's married to Cleopas. I was
there at the crucifixion, holding up Jesus' mother Mary as
a sword pierced her soul, brutal inch by brutal inch.

TODAY WE WERE WALKING HOME TO EMMAUS. When I say
walking, it was more like dragging ourselves. More than
once I felt like lying down on the edge of the road and
never moving again. I don't think I have ever felt so weary
and hopeless in all my life. I don't really know what I'd
been expecting. But it wasn't this. Jesus was the kind of
person who gave you such hope – in him, in the world, in
yourself – and I knew that if I could just be near him that
hope would grow and grow and never stop.

We had hoped that he would redeem Israel. Now I think
about it, I'm not really sure what I thought that meant. He
didn't have the look to be a military leader. I don't mean
he was all meek and mild – he could rage with the best of
them, and did often. It was more that brandishing a sword
wasn't his style. I suppose I imagined the whole host of
heaven would come down and drive out the Romans as in
the stories of old. I realize how daft it sounds now I say it
out loud, but I did believe he could. I did believe he would.
So this morning, after everything that had happened, we

packed our bags and went home. I thought it was a bit soon. But on that long, awful day on Friday, I watched my hope ebb away with every dying breath he took. And then the women came this morning to tell us the tomb was empty, saying something hair-brained about him being risen from the dead. And we'd rushed outside and seen the world exactly as it had always been, Roman soldiers and all. The fight went out of me and we packed up and left.

It was Cleopas who started the row. He started by grumbling that I'd been the one to follow that Jesus in the first place. If it hadn't been for me, he'd have been comfortably at home right now. That did it. I let him have it. All my pent-up anger and hurt and bitterness spewed out over him in a massive tidal wave.

I was taking a breath for the second wave when I became aware of a stranger just standing there, smiling at us, asking what we were talking about.

Cleopas glared at him in disbelief.

'Are you the only one who has no idea what has been going on?'

The stranger smiled again.

'Maybe I am. Why don't you tell me about it while we walk?'

So we did. Turn and turnabout, we told him about our hopes and our fears, about Jesus and what he'd meant to us. Stranger though he was, I found myself telling him things

I'd never imagined saying out loud. We even told him about the story the women had told this morning about him being alive. He listened and nodded, and listened and nodded.

Then suddenly he said, 'How stupid you are and slow to catch on.'

I thought it was a bit rude, frankly. But then he began telling us about the Scriptures. And I forgot to be annoyed. Starting at the very beginning, he laid it all out. He told my story – all my hopes and my dreams – in the words of the Scriptures. My heart leapt and burned within me.

I was so totally and utterly absorbed that I was amazed to hear him saying, 'Look, your village is just down there. I'll leave you here and travel on.'

We had travelled seven miles, it felt, in an instant. All of a sudden, I couldn't bear the thought that this stranger might leave us. It felt as though I'd known him all my life. It seemed Cleopas felt the same, and so we begged and cajoled, pleaded and persuaded him to eat with us. Eventually he gave in and came with us.

I'd brought food back with us from Jerusalem, so it was only a matter of minutes before we were ready to eat. It was, I remember thinking, a bit forward of him to take the bread and bless it. That was Cleopas' job as host. But the thought had gone as soon as it half-formed in my mind. The arms of the man's tunic slipped downwards as he raised his hands, revealing gaping holes in each wrist.

And the words … the words of blessing and gratitude to his Father in heaven were words I'd heard every single day for the past few years – words he'd said every time he took bread and blessed it. I looked at the bread in my hand, and in that moment I knew, I knew it was him.

He's alive. He is alive. He is alive.

Cleopas' mouth formed the words faster than mine did, 'You're al–'.

But he was gone – the loaf falling to the plate with a crash.

We sprang to our feet and ran quicker than I could ever have imagined was possible, our feet beating out the rhythm as we went:

He's alive, he's alive, he's alive.

WE ARRIVED IN JERUSALEM, hot and breathless.

'I thought you went home?' said Peter. Voices around the room chimed in.

'So did we …'

'You might have said goodbye …'

'You can't just go off like that …'

I was still panting, trying to catch my breath, unable to speak.

'We've got news,' said Peter.

Mary – yes, *that* one, the one you are thinking about, Jesus' mother – spoke quietly, but her voice cut through all the hubbub.

'If you give them a moment, I think you'll find they have, too.'

Ascension
Day

Mary, Mother of Jesus' Story

M Y NAME IS MARY. Yes, that one; the one you're thinking of, Mary, Jesus' mother.

I never thought I'd find myself here, sitting among so many people who'd followed my son – Peter, John, James, Salome, Mary from Magdala, Mary (Clopas' wife) and so many others. None of us ever thought we'd be here, least of all me. But here we are and now we have to work out what we do now that he's gone.

I got used to him going over the years. People tell you that there's none so close as a mother and her eldest son. I'd look around Nazareth and see the women with their sons.

'Have you seen how my son has grown?' they would ask.

'Have I told you how clever my son is?'

'My son, my son …'

The words would follow me as I went about my daily routine. Sometimes they would wait for me to respond with tales of 'my son', but the words wouldn't quite form in me. You see he never felt truly and entirely mine: my possession to own and show off.

Even from the start he never was completely mine. Just after he was born, when I was battered and torn, weary from childbirth, when all I wanted to do was close my eyes and hold him against my heart so that we would be one flesh again, like we were when he was in my womb. Even then, strangers came – smelling of night air, and sheep's wool and other things I didn't care to identify – telling me they'd come to see the saviour, the Messiah, the Lord. And then there were those three from the East, wafting altogether different scents like perfume and burial spices, as well as gold, which has no smell at all. Not to forget that time in the Temple, when Simeon took him out of my arms entirely and told me a sword would pierce my soul, and the elderly prophet Anna declared he'd come to redeem Israel. So, no, even at the start when we should have been wrapped up together, learning to know each other, he wasn't completely mine and he hasn't been ever since.

As a child he would slide away from the group, and we would go looking for him, Joseph and I, and we'd find him on his own, looking upwards or outwards to the horizon, a pensive look on his face, his lips silently forming words we couldn't hear.

I learned over the years to let him go. He needed the space, the time on his own, and I learned to give it to him. So much so that one awful year we lost him completely. We'd been to Jerusalem for the festival and were travelling back home. Slowly we realized that not only was he not with us, he wasn't with anyone. We ran back to the Temple, and there he was in the grand court of women, surrounded by learned men, talking to them like he was one of them.

'Didn't you know I'd be in my Father's house?' he asked.

Well, no, we didn't. How could we have known?

That was him. Always slipping away, always unknowable. Don't get me wrong: I know that he loved me. Sometimes I thought he might even love me more than those other boys loved their mothers. I could see his love in his eyes but it felt as though he was teaching me to love him with

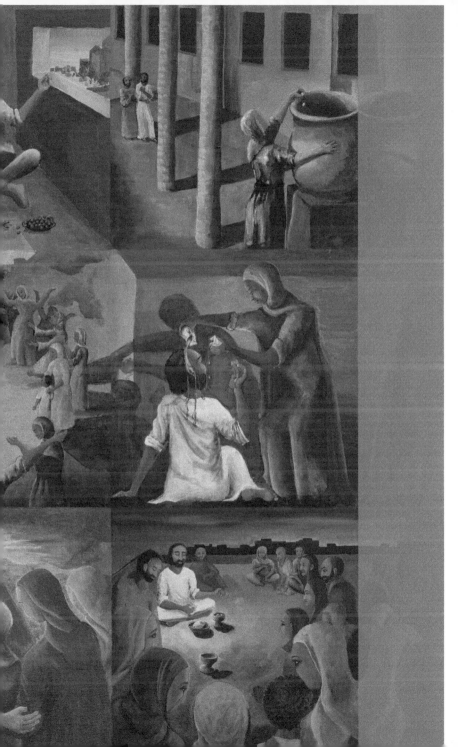

every fibre of my being, and, in loving him, to let him go, to let him be. It was a lesson I had to learn again and again. He loved me as I loved him, but he wasn't mine. He had come, he said, later on, for the whole world – he loved us, all of us – but he didn't belong to us, we didn't own him.

The last of the lessons, the most brutal of all, I learned on a dark, gloomy hillside outside Jerusalem. By then I had got used to letting him go. I was used to him travelling around Galilee and even into the Decapolis. I was used to him teaching large crowds and calling them his mother and brothers and sisters. I was even used to the thought of him going to Jerusalem when the leaders were baying for his blood. I thought I had got used to letting him go, but I had one final lesson to learn, the hardest one of all. I had to stand and watch while he died.

It's come in handy, this lesson, over the past forty days since he rose again. In our joy we wanted to wrap him in love, to keep him with us safely within reach and never let him go again.

Mary – the one from Magdala – had seen him first. She came to me later, tears in her eyes, telling me how he had called her by name and how she had known in that moment that it was him. But, she'd said, he'd told her not to cling on to him.

'I don't understand,' she'd sobbed, her head on my lap, 'I just want him to know how much I love him.'

I stroked her hair, pondering all the lessons I'd learnt over the years and then tried to explain. That loving him means allowing him to be who he is. That love so often seeks to possess and to limit, but his love – real love – is freeing not possessing, permitting not limiting. That loving him doesn't give us rights over him; loving him doesn't let us say who he is or what he came to be.

Then, one by one, the others came, and one by one I tried to teach them my hard-learned lesson. I'd had years to learn it, but they had to learn it in a few days.

It's just as well I did, really. Not long ago, the men came saying that they thought he'd really gone for good this time. One moment they were talking to him and the next he was rising upwards. A cloud hid him from sight, and then he was gone.

They had all stood there gazing at the spot where he'd been – their brains struggling to catch up – when an angel appeared and told them that this time he really had gone back to heaven.

So here I am in the middle of them all, with them looking at me expectantly, waiting for me to tell them what we do now ... now that he's gone. I look at them and feel my heart lurch with love, they look so lost and lonely, not knowing what to do.

I ponder for a while. I've done a lot of that over the years, pondering. After all, there has been a lot to ponder about. Then suddenly I know. Suddenly I know exactly what to say.

'My children,' I say – because in a way they are now my children, all of them. 'My children, we love him, we let him go, and then we wait.'

'What are we waiting for?'

That's Peter, always swifter to the question than any of the others.

'I don't know,' I say. 'But what I do know is that he won't leave us entirely alone. He never does, he never would. If we pray and wait, and wait and pray, something will happen. We'll know it when we see it.'

'What if we miss it?' asks Thomas, as full of anxiety as Peter was of questions.

'This time,' I say, 'this time I think that that is very unlikely.'

Notes and Resources

Miriam's Story

Bible passages
Psalm 118 and Mark 11.1-11

Questions

- Are there any parts of Psalm 118 that jump out at you as particularly helpful for understanding what was going on when Jesus entered Jerusalem?
- When the crowd on the road to Jerusalem hailed Jesus and shouted 'Hosanna!', what do you think they imagined was happening?
- Why do you think they, apparently, changed their minds so quickly so that by the end of the week they were calling for Jesus to be crucified?

It might help you to know ...

Psalm 118

Psalms 113–118 are known as the Hallel Psalms and in later Jewish tradition were read before, during and after the Passover meal, though it is not clear whether this association had been made at the time of Jesus. Psalm 118 was, however, a psalm that was widely associated with messianic expectation and the hopes of someone who would come to vindicate and save Israel. Many scholars think that Psalm 118 was a dramatic psalm in which different voices spoke. There is the voice of a king recalling a near disaster in battle, which, at the last moment, was transformed by God into a victory. There are the voices of the crowd who had come with the king to the Temple, and there are the voices of the priests who welcome the king into the Temple and bless the king 'who comes in the name of the Lord'.

If the pilgrims, on the road to Jerusalem, had begun singing this psalm of messianic expectation, it would not have taken much of a leap to see Jesus as this long-awaited Messiah king. The most striking feature of this psalm is that the priests welcome the king into the Temple. In Mark 11.11, Jesus arrived in Jerusalem, went to the Temple, looked around and left again. The lack of welcome for him was stark.

Hosanna

The word hosanna is well known in Christian hymnody and songs but in the Bible it occurs only in this story in the Gospels. That is because it is a direct quote of a Hebrew word used in Psalm 118. The Hebrew word *hoshea na* if put into Greek letters (but not translated), turns into hosanna. In Hebrew it means 'save now' (see Psalm 118.25), but over time it became a shout of praise because people were so confident that God would save them. The question for us is whether we think the cry in the story of the entry into Jerusalem was closer to a shout of praise or a plea for help, or indeed both.

Sarah's Story

Bible passages
Mark 11.27–12.34 (or you could just read Mark 12.28-34)

Questions

- Love God and love your neighbour – what does this mean for us in practice as we seek to follow Jesus' teaching?
- Jesus is asked questions by all sorts of people during this last week of his life, but the exchange with the scribe is different and feels less confrontational. What can we learn from this exchange about how we ask questions?
- What do you think Jesus meant when he said, 'You are not far from the Kingdom of God'?

It might help you to know ...

Jesus and the Temple

It is easy to miss the fact that, following the entry into Jerusalem and the cleansing of the Temple, Jesus spent most of the following week back in the Temple talking with the Chief Priest and his allies (Mark 11.27–12.12), Pharisees and Herodians (Mark 12.13-17), Sadducees (Mark 12.18-27), and a single scribe (12.28-34). References such as 12.35, 'While he was teaching in the temple ...', make clear that all these conversations took place in the Temple precincts. This is worth thinking about when we reflect on the meaning and significance of the cleansing of the Temple – whatever Jesus did it did not preclude him from spending most of the rest of the week there.

When we talk about Jesus teaching in the Temple it is probable that he was in the Royal Stoa or Portico along the southern wall of the Temple mount. When Herod the Great rebuilt the Temple, he expanded its size considerably. In particular, he added a large basilica on to the southern wall of the Temple complex. This was a covered colonnaded area four columns deep and 40 columns in length, opening on one side into the Temple precincts. The teaching that took place in the Temple would have happened in the Royal Stoa.

Scribes

We are very familiar with a group known as 'scribes' from the Gospels but it is not entirely clear who they were. Their title implies that they can read and write, which is important in a largely non-literate society. Conversations, such as the one in Mark 12.28-34, indicate that they also knew the law inside out. As a result, many scholars suggest that the scribes were off-duty priests and Levites. Priests and Levites were split into 24 divisions and, in addition to being on duty during the three major festivals (Passover, Weeks or Pentecost, and Tabernacles), they would serve in the Temple for two weeks a year.

The best explanation for what they did for the rest of the time is that they were scribes in their local villages, reading and writing for people who could not, interpreting the law for those who needed it, declaring people clean or unclean as necessary, and so on.

Anna's Story

Bible passages
Luke 2:22-38 and Mark 12.38-44

Questions

- Does reading Jesus' condemnation of the scribes who 'devour widows' houses' before the story of the widow with her two coins make any difference to how you read this story?
- Why do you think Jesus was so complimentary about the widow who gave everything she had to live on?
- What might it have felt like to be a woman – like the widow in this story – who couldn't go further in the Temple than the court of women?

It might help you to know ...

Women and the last week of Jesus' life
One of the striking features of the stories of the last week of Jesus' life is that most of them take place in the Temple and most of them feature some sort of conflict or misunderstanding of who Jesus is. Two stories stand out against this backdrop: the story of the widow with her two coins and the story of the woman with the costly perfume. Both of these women act out of devotion and generosity, rather than suspicion and defensiveness.

The treasury boxes and the Temple tax
Herod's Temple was made up of three key areas. By far and away the largest area was the court of the Gentiles where

animals could be bought for sacrifice or money changed from the Roman denarii into the Tyrian silver needed for the Temple tax. From there one could proceed into the court of the women, also known as the treasury. This was as far as women could go, since beyond that was the court of the priests (where the sacrifices took place) and beyond that the sanctuary and the Holy of Holies.

The treasury consisted of thirteen collection boxes, two specially dedicated for the collection of the Temple tax, and eleven others. The collection boxes were trumpet-shaped receptacles, the top of which was made of bronze so you would be able to hear the coins clink as they dropped. Women were not liable to pay Temple tax. Temple tax, a half shekel for each adult male, was paid by all men over the age of 20 in addition to the general tithe of 10 per cent. Temple tax had to be paid in special coinage – Tyrian silver, which was 95 per cent silver. The description of the money paid to Judas as silver coins make it likely he was paid in Temple tax coinage – money that should have been used for the upkeep of the Temple.

The coins the widow gave were two 'lepta'. Lepta were Roman coins of the smallest denomination possible. They were made of copper and were tiny. There was no obligation on the widow to give any money at all, and certainly not two coins. The implication of the story is that she could have given just one and still been generous, but the giving of two coins suggested that she was giving everything she had.

Susannah's Story

Bible passages

Matthew 26.6-13; Mark 14.3-9; Luke 7.36-50;
John 12.1-8 (or just Mark 14.3-9)

Questions

- Do you think the different accounts of the anointing of Jesus reflect one event told in different ways, or more than one event? (If you feel inspired to explore this, compare Luke 7.36-50 with Mark 14.3-9).
- Why do you think the woman wanted to anoint Jesus? What was she trying to say by doing it?
- What do you think Jesus meant when he said, 'Wherever the good news is proclaimed in the whole world, what she has done will be told in remembrance of her'? Has this, in fact, been the case?

It might help you to know ...

One woman or four? (Or maybe two or three?)
Each Gospel has an account of a woman anointing Jesus but the stories themselves are quite different from each other. Matthew and Mark's accounts are closest to each other. In them, an unnamed woman anointed Jesus' head with costly oil; in Luke and John, a woman (in Luke a sinner; in John Mary, sister of Lazarus and Martha) anointed Jesus' feet with oil. In Mathew, Mark and John, Jesus was in Bethany; in Luke the location is not recorded. In Matthew, Mark and Luke, Jesus' host was called Simon (though he was either

a leper or a Pharisee); in John, Jesus' host was Lazarus. The combinations of overlaps and differences make it hard to decide whether this is an account recording one event or more than one. I usually opt for more than one, but in this story I wanted to introduce the question of what a woman with a reputation for being a 'sinner' might have experienced and so explored that as a background to the story.

Costly oil in alabaster jars

Alabaster was well known as a receptacle for costly perfume in the ancient world. Its opaque quality ensured that the perfume did not go off. Alabaster jars were often sealed to further ensure long life but could be broken at the neck to get the perfume out. The word used for 'broke open' the jar in Mark 14.3, however, suggests that the woman smashed the whole jar rather than just at the neck. It is Mark and John's Gospels that identify which kind of perfume the woman used. The description 'nard' refers to oil from the spikenard plant which, now as then, can be harvested from the foothills of the Himalayas.

Some think that alabaster jars were most commonly given to the daughters of wealthy families on the occasion of their betrothal.

The court of Herod Antipas

In this story I make mention of the court of Herod Antipas. Antipas was one of the sons of Herod the Great who ruled over Galilee and Perea from 4 BC to AD 39. He, and his court, had a reputation for immorality and cruelty.

Indeed, John the Baptist was killed when he criticized the marriage of Herodias to Herod Antipas on the grounds that she had been previously married to Herod Antipas' brother Herod II. On one level this was the least of the problems – Herodias' daughter by Herod II, Salome, was married to Philip, another of Herod the Great's sons, and Salome's half-uncle.

Joanna's Story

Bible passage
Mark 14.12-25

Questions
- Jesus seemed to know someone in Jerusalem well enough to 'pre-book' a guest room. Do you have any reflections on how he did this? (Hint: there is no right answer to this – it asks you to use your imagination!)
- What do you imagine the Last Supper was like? What do you think the first disciples who were there thought was going on?
- Do you think the disciples had any idea of what was about to happen at this point?

It might help you to know …

Joanna, wife of Chuza

A person called Joanna is named twice in Luke's Gospel: once in Luke 8.3, where she is listed alongside Mary Magdalene, Susannah and 'many others who provided for them out of their resources', and once in Luke 24.10 where it was reported that she was one of the witnesses to the resurrection. Apart from this we know very little about her at all, though the nature of the references do suggest that she was a disciple of Jesus.

The Last Supper

The influence of great artwork through the centuries encourages us to imagine only Jesus and the twelve as present at the Last Supper, sitting on chairs at a large dining-type table. Mark's account suggests to us that this mental image is incorrect. Jesus sent two disciples ahead to prepare the Passover meal (14.13) and then arrived later with the twelve (14.17). As a result, there were at least fifteen people present if not more. Given that we know from passages like Luke 8.1-3 that Jesus had female disciples as well as male it seems at least possible that there were women present.

Jesus instructed his two disciples to ask for the 'guest room', which is later described as 'large' and 'upstairs' (14.14). It is impossible to know where the room was or what it was like. However, given that space was at a premium in Jerusalem and given the climate, it is known that a number of guest rooms were located on the roof. I have opted to imagine this in my story here.

Tiberias

The city of Tiberias was built on the shores of the sea of Galilee by Herod Antipas around the year AD 20. He named it after the second emperor of the Roman Empire, Tiberius Caesar Augustus. Its mild winters and clement summers made it a desirable place to live.

Salome's Story

Bible passages

Mark 15.1-41 and John 19.17-37 (or just John 19.17-37)

Questions

- Why do you think that the women, who had followed Jesus, felt able to go to the crucifixion when the men did not?
- John's Gospel makes much of Jesus handing his mother into the care of the beloved disciple. Why do you think this is? (There are various ways you might answer this.)
- What difference does it make to know that a group of women were there at Jesus' crucifixion?

It might help you to know ...

Salome

Although the name Salome is commonly associated with the daughter of Herodias who danced for Herod Antipas in exchange for the head of John the Baptist, she is never called by name in the Gospel accounts (Mark 6.21-29; Matthew 14.6-11). It is the ancient Jewish historian Josephus who identifies her as Salome. There is, however, a 'Salome' mentioned by Mark in Mark 15.40 and 16.1 as one of the group of women who were there at the crucifixion and then later at the resurrection.

Burial customs in first-century Judaism

Although most knowledge of burial customs comes from texts written much later than the first century, it seems to have been the custom for men to oversee the burial rites of men. These involved anointing the body and wrapping it in linen and spices. A key element for a 'good burial' was to be buried in a tomb with one's ancestors. As a result, many burials were in a burial chamber often carved out of rock. These had 'shelves' around the side of the space on which bodies would be placed. Later, when more space was needed, the bones would be placed in an ossuary but kept in the same chamber.

One of the significances of Jesus being buried in a new tomb was that it meant there were no other bodies in the tomb. Thus, at the resurrection, the tomb was truly empty.

Mary Magdalene's Story

Bible passages

John 20.1-18 (and, if you have time, John 10.1-6)

Questions

- One of the odd features of John's account of the resurrection is that Peter and the beloved disciple came and saw the empty tomb but then went away again. Why might they have done this?
- Why do you think that Mary didn't recognize Jesus when she first saw him?
- Discuss the importance of Jesus calling Mary by her name. If you have time, compare it to John 10.1-6 and the shepherd calling sheep by their names.

It might help you to know ...

Mary Magdalene

Although Mary Magdalene is commonly depicted as a prostitute, there is nothing in the Gospels to suggest this at all. Her name suggests that she came from a city called Magdala, which, until the building of Tiberias by Herod Antipas, was the biggest and most wealthy city on the sea of Galilee. Most of what is known about Mary in the Gospels comes from Luke 8, which described the women who helped support Jesus from their own resources, of whom one was 'Mary, called Magdalene, from whom seven demons had gone out'. This suggests that Mary had her own means with which to support Jesus.

The connection with prostitution came via a subsequent conflation of all four of the accounts of the woman anointing Jesus with oil and the transference of the name of Mary of Bethany on to Mary Magdalene.

Known by name
One of the lovely details of John's account of the resurrection is Jesus' calling of Mary by her name. This picks up the detail of the 'good shepherd' from John 10.1-6, who not only called the sheep but knew them by name. As the story indicates, the custom of calling sheep was widespread in the Middle East – and remains common today. Sheep were regularly kept overnight altogether in a large sheep pen, but in the morning the shepherds of the different flocks would stand and call and the sheep, recognizing the voice of their own shepherd, would gather round them. This custom is reflected in John 10.1-6 and implied again in John 20.16.

Mary, Wife of Clopas' Story

Bible passage
Luke 24.13-35

Questions

- If they had heard the news of Jesus' resurrection, why do you think the two disciples were going home so despondently?
- What do you think Jesus might have said to them when he was interpreting 'the things about himself in all the scriptures'?
- What changed in the two disciples to enable them to recognize Jesus?

It might help you to know ...

The identity of the two disciples

Nearly all artwork depicting the road to Emmaus features two male disciples. There is nothing in the text to suggest this. One disciple is named but the other is unnamed. It is at least possible – maybe even highly likely – that two disciples travelling to the same house together were a married couple.

Indeed, it is interesting that John's Gospel (19.25) mentions a Mary, the wife of Clopas, a name quite similar to Cleopas. It is possible that Cleopas' companion, then, was the Mary mentioned by John's Gospel.

'Talking'

Another factor to note here is that Luke suggests that the couple were arguing. The words used escalate much more in Greek than in the usual English translations. Verse 14 ('and talking with each other') used the verb *homileō* which means to converse. Verse 15 ('they were talking and discussing') repeats *homileō* but then uses *suzēteō* a verb more commonly used for debate or argue. When, in verse 17, Jesus asked them what they were talking about he used the verb *antiballō* (to throw against), suggesting that they were having a row.

Mary, Mother of Jesus' Story

Bible passage
Acts 1.12-14

Questions
- What range of emotions might the disciples have experienced after the Ascension?
- Discuss Mary's presence among the disciples in the upper room. What kinds of things might they have said to her, and she to them?
- What do you think they were praying about?

CPSIA information can be obtained
at www.ICGtesting.com
Printed in the USA
BVHW010526230422
634907BV00017BA/259